# Endure

Tori Gatke

BookLeaf Publishing

Presentation by *BookLeaf Publishing*

Web: www.bookleafpub.com

E-mail: info@bookleafpub.com

ISBN: 9789357213561

First edition 2023

# Strike the Chords

You played with me like a child plays with a piano
Acting erratically, you would sometimes strike true
One right move and I would sing a ballad
You loved it when I sang, the louder the better
But more often than not, your meaty fingers missed the mark
Each time it ripped a cry from my throat
But this pleased you too
After all, sound is sound
The volume is what matters
That's what you were taught
As blows rained down on my heart
My cries grew softer until they stopped
There was no point in screaming
You would just keep going

So I sat
I took your clumsy attempts at love
And I stayed quiet
But this brought forth a hurricane
Your pudgy feet kicking at nothing
Crocodile tears raining from your eyes

You wailed until I was sure your lungs would burst, but they didn't
And I stayed quiet
Finally, your storm faded and you looked at me
For the first time you noticed my wood was splintered and my keys were chipped
You hit me one last time, just to be sure
And I stayed quiet
Then you got up and toddled away
Off to find another toy
Someone else to ruin

# Quell

Whether I am needed to lead or to follow,
let me be a guide.
Send forth your strongest,
and let me guide them to where they are needed
most;
Send forth your weakest,
and let me guide them to where they may find
help;
Send forth your youngest,
and let me guide them to the brightest possible
future;
Send forth your lost,
and let me guide them to a home where they
may thrive;
Send forth your pain,
and let me guide you through your storms;
Send forth yourself,
and let me guide you as I wish I had let someone
guide me.
If I am not needed to forge the new path,
let me walk beside those who do.
Let me quell the pain and the sorrow.

# Eyes

Her eyes are a scene out of a fairy tale
The river where the forest meets the mountains
Late dawn on the first day of true sun in winter
Gentle beams of sun cause fresh snow to glow
The frozen river has been breached from below
Uneven shards of ice, like crystals, glitter there
This beauty
This majesty
This wonder
All dwell in her eyes

# The Bowl

Wooden and smoothed by working hands
In the earthy dusky room that night
The kitchen where the flour became bread
Outside is the pump inside is the home
A woven basket of berries next to the bowl
Blackberries bursting to bleed and stain
Dropped inside in a loose rambling pile
Tepid water growing colder without sun
Poured in and slowly poured back out
Clean steady hands long used to work
Reach in and crush with a gentleness
Until all there is is everything and nothing
Red blood staining worn hands
Black and red so deep it might as well be
Specks of white reveal missed seeds
But also look like the appearing stars
Constellations, galaxies, and supernovas
All appears in the swirling black red
Globs of the flesh from the fruit float by
The asteroids we can't see but know exist
Flesh torn up leaving blood on the hands
The hands of an aging woman doing work
Work to keep the universe in the bowl

# Burn

Outside I smile
But inside I burn
I hide it all away
And keep it in
Bury it down
Ignore the pain
But it's still there
Right here in me
Where it started
All of the heat
All of the pressure
No matter how hard
I try to ignore it
I can't escape it
I don't know how
To deal with it
So I just smile
While I burn

# Waiting

I am not a being,
I am the wind in the trees
and the sun on the waves,
yet here I am trapped
in this unfitting casket of flesh
far younger than my primal self.
Out of nothing beyond desperation
I surround this prison
with woods tall and dark and knowing.
Even with the wind biting at my shell
and I myself fighting from within,
I know this to be futile.
It is not enough.
It will never be enough.
Nothing can ever break open the casket,
but amongst the ancient forces
of the Mother of All,
I allow myself to dream
of being free--truly free.
Are others like me,
I ponder,
trapped in a vessel
unable to keep pace
with their nature
or am I the lone fighter

in this vast superficial world?
Inside of me,
power whirls and screams
while outside I lay unmoving
on an uneven bed of leaves
and soil ensconced by mournful trees.
As waves slowly eat away the cliff side,
I wish I could eat through this Hell.
I would scream for help,
but no being can save me.
Instead, I whisper to the wind,
I cry to the stars,
and await the Mother's response.
I am waiting still.

# This Side Of My Skin

This side of my skin wasn't enough.
You didn't care about
The fire in my heart
Or the gold in my veins,
The strength in my bones
Or the beauty in my brain.
That wasn't enough.
All you cared about was
The gloss of my hair
And the bow of my lips,
The flash of my eyes
And the curve of my hips.
This side of my skin just wasn't enough.

# I Learned

I learned how to fly
By being thrown out the nest
I learned how to sing rather than cry
Sweet, chirping notes drowning the pain
I learned how to hurt time and again
Thanks to having these hollow bones
In the end, I learned not to trust anyone at all

# Can You Blame Me

I outgrew the pond
And dove into the sea,
But now I'm just prey.
The smallest fish
In the biggest pond.
So when I saw the bait,
All shining and promising,
I took it.
I shouldn't have.
But how can you blame me?
Just surviving
Never thriving
Always on guard and in pain.
Suddenly, an escape!
Glittering and hopeful.
What would you have done?
The escape turned out to be
Jumping from the frying pan
And straight into the fire,
But can you blame me for trying?

# Ablaze

No one expects an angel to set the world on fire
but they should
No one soul can bear the weight of wings for
long
Being an angel is a sentence of ruin
The pressure mounts far too fast
Soft white feathers with golden rachis outweigh
iron shackles
For shackles can be broken with no outrage, no
resentment, no shame
The very tides will shift if wings are lost
For any rhyme or reason
No one appears to care why
No one appears to care how
When an angel loses their wings, they are to
blame
The pressure on the soul mounts the longer the
wings are worn
And one day
Maybe not today
Maybe not tomorrow
They will crack
When they crack
Oh beware that day
For it will be an angel who sets the world ablaze

# The River

Take my hand
Let me lead you
Dancing through the river
We'll run down
To where the water's shallow
We'll dance and play
Sing songs of "I love you"s
If you take my hand
And let me lead you
Out of town to where
All is green and blue
No one will see us
As we twirl and sway together
Kissed by the rain
And held by the wind
Take my hand
Let me lead you
Dancing through the river

# Rage

Rage isn't a fire; it's the sun
Beating down
Hot, oppressive, exhausting
At first it feels powerful and safe
But then it drains you completely
Sometimes you bask in the warmth
So long everything else feels cold
Bask even longer, and you burn
The solution is not to avoid the sun
But to feel it
No hiding, no basking, just feeling

# Curiosity

From counting stars
In the Garden of Eden
To fearing all
In the world of Man

It was just an apple,
What harm could one bite do?

From a life unbothered
In a state of naivete
To torment and pain
In an unforgiving world

It was just a box,
What harm could one peek do?

I've heard time and again
Curiosity killed the cat
But isn't satisfaction
Supposed to bring it back?

# Mirror

I looked in the mirror
But I didn't see me
I saw you
Smiling at me
That soft smile
That melts my heart
I didn't see the shock
On my own face
I didn't see the tears
Even when they dropped
All I saw was you
You looked at me and saw
Something no one else did
You showed me who I was
And who I am
So now
When I look in the mirror
All I can see is you

# Stardust

Once upon a time, I was radiant
I was serene
I was perfect
I always did as I was told
And colored inside the lines

Until one day,
It all became too much
Pressures compounded
Heat intensified
Far too fast

Then I was
Broken and
Battered and
Beaten and
Shattered

In my darkest hour I was
Found by Moonlight
Readied by Time
Forged by Fire
Remade by Passion

From strangers
To family
They took me in
They built me up
They let me out

I’ve been
Compromised
Eviscerated
Pulverized
And devastated

Yet here I remain,
Lifted back up
By Strength
After falling from Grace
Into Doubt

Not the same
Not quite who I was
No longer flesh
Made of Stardust instead
And now I will shine.

# I'm Sorry

I set myself alight to keep you warm
But now I've burned out
I stretched myself thin to keep you whole
But now there's little left of me
I filled your cup before I filled my own
But now there's none for me
I gave you all I could and more
But now I have to stop

# Zip-Ties

My life is in pieces
Shattered and tattered
I'm holding it together
With Zip Ties and Hope

Plastic and feelings
Holding together
Everything that's left
Of who I was

Maybe it's time
To cut the ties
Mourn the dream
And move on

My life isn't over
There's time to grow
But I have to move on
Before it's too late

# Goddess

Delicate fingers manipulate
One thousand languid shadows
Beneath a sea of raw power
Whispers soar as rose petals
Of my goddess of eternity

A lovely woman
Smelling of peach
With moonlight skin
Beautiful friend
My diamond

# Leaves

Leaves of green
among which we sit
Match your eyes
but not in color
Healthy, full of life,
both gentle and strong

Leaves of faded yellows
dance between us
In time with music
we can’t hear
Like the butterflies
in my stomach

Leaves of muddled browns
lie beneath my feet
You have fallen
from my heart all the same
But these memories
will feed a new start.

# Atlas

Atlas, which is worse
the weight of the world
or of those you cannot help?
Are your true struggles
the ones you can see
or the ones you can't?
Why do you refuse to give up
even on your darkest days?
Where does your strength come from
and what do you stand for?
Does it hurt
to bear the burdens
of others on your shoulders?
Oh Atlas, you have no choice
But I do
And I want out.

# Silver

I am made of neither gold nor stone
I am made of silver
Silver as singing flutes
Silver as deadly blades
Silver as the moon
And like the moon
Sometimes I go dark
Sometimes I shine bright
But night after night, I rise again
And I always will

www.ingramcontent.com/pod-product-compliance
Lightning Source LLC
Chambersburg PA
CBHW051719130826
49812CB00034B/1263
*9789357213561*